Cat Breeds

EXOTIC SHORTHAIRS

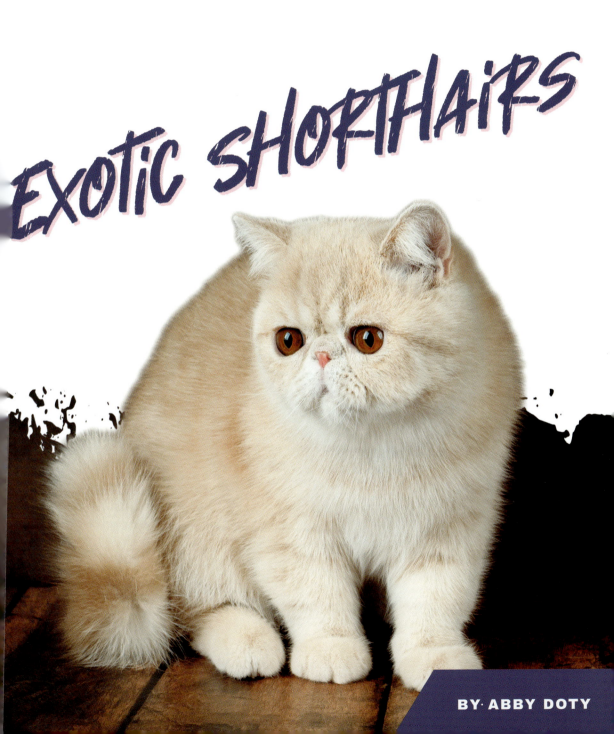

BY ABBY DOTY

WWW.APEXEDITIONS.COM

Copyright © 2025 by Apex Editions, Mendota Heights, MN 55120. All rights reserved. No part of this book may be reproduced or utilized in any form or by any means without written permission from the publisher.

Apex is distributed by North Star Editions:
sales@northstareditions.com | 888-417-0195

Produced for Apex by Red Line Editorial.

Photographs ©: Shutterstock Images, cover, 1, 4–5, 6–7, 10–11, 12, 13, 14, 15, 16–17, 18, 20–21, 22–23, 24, 26, 27, 29; iStockphoto, 8–9

Library of Congress Control Number: 2024943626

ISBN
979-8-89250-310-5 (hardcover)
979-8-89250-348-8 (paperback)
979-8-89250-423-2 (ebook pdf)
979-8-89250-386-0 (hosted ebook)

Printed in the United States of America
Mankato, MN
012025

NOTE TO PARENTS AND EDUCATORS
Apex books are designed to build literacy skills in striving readers. Exciting, high-interest content attracts and holds readers' attention. The text is carefully leveled to allow students to achieve success quickly. Additional features, such as bolded glossary words for difficult terms, help build comprehension.

TABLE OF CONTENTS

CHAPTER 1
CUDDLY CAT 4

CHAPTER 2
MIXED BREED 10

CHAPTER 3
CUTE CATS 16

CHAPTER 4
CAT CARE 22

COMPREHENSION QUESTIONS • 28
GLOSSARY • 30
TO LEARN MORE • 31
ABOUT THE AUTHOR • 31
INDEX • 32

CHAPTER 1

CUDDLY CAT

An exotic shorthair naps in a sunny spot. Suddenly, his ears **prick** up. The cat hears his owner shake a jingle ball.

Exotic shorthairs spend lots of time lying around.

The owner rolls the ball across the floor. The cat stands up and stretches. Then, he runs after the ball.

APARTMENT LIVING

Exotic shorthairs can be great pets for people who live in apartments. The cats are not very active. So, they don't need a lot of space to move around. They also don't meow often.

Exotic shorthairs tend to play in short bursts.

The owner tosses the ball a few more times. Then, she sits down to read a book. The cat jumps onto her lap. He curls up and takes another nap.

FAST FACT

Exotic shorthairs often follow their owners from room to room.

Many exotic shorthairs love to cuddle.

CHAPTER 2

MIXED BREED

In the 1950s, people wanted American shorthair cats to have silver fur and green eyes. To get this look, **breeders** had American shorthairs **mate** with Persian cats.

American shorthairs are active and playful cats.

However, the kittens ended up looking like short-haired Persian cats. Even so, many people liked this look. They decided to make a new Persian-like **breed**.

Persian cats have round, flat faces and long, fluffy fur.

Like Persians, exotic shorthairs have round heads and big paws.

EASY CARE

Many people like how Persian cats look. But the cats' long fur must be brushed every day. Exotic shorthairs look **similar** to Persians. But their shorter fur is easier to care for.

Exotics are more active and playful than Persians.

People called the new type of cat exotic shorthairs. The breed quickly spread around the world. Exotic shorthairs became popular pets.

FAST FACT

At first, all exotics had silver fur. Today, they come in many colors.

Exotic shorthairs' coats often have two or more colors.

CHAPTER 3

CUTE CATS

Exotic shorthairs are medium-sized cats. Most weigh about 11 pounds (5 kg). The cats have short legs and big paws.

Exotic shorthairs are usually 10 to 12 inches (25 to 30 cm) tall.

Exotic shorthairs have small ears and round faces. They have short tails. The cats' fur is soft and thick.

FLAT FACES

Like Persian cats, exotic shorthairs have short muzzles. Their flat noses can cause breathing problems. Flat-faced cats may also overheat. They cannot pant easily to cool off.

◀ Exotics have small nostrils. The cats may have trouble getting air through the openings.

Most exotic shorthairs are friendly and calm. They are sweet and snuggly with people. And they get along well with other pets.

FAST FACT

Exotic shorthairs may be shy at first. Some need time to get used to strangers.

Living with other animals can help exotic shorthairs stay calm while their owners are away.

CHAPTER 4

CAT CARE

Exotic shorthairs do not need as much grooming as Persians. But their fur should still be brushed once a week. Owners should also use a damp cloth to clean near the cats' eyes. That way, tears won't **stain** the cats' fur.

Exotic shorthairs tend to shed most during spring. The cats may need more brushing during this time.

Exotic shorthairs can be alone for a few hours. But owners should spend time with their cats every day.

 CALM CATS

Most exotic shorthairs get along with families. But many prefer living in quiet places. So, the cats often do well in families with older children.

◀ **Owners can leave out toys for their exotics to play with when alone.**

Exotic shorthairs need 15 to 30 minutes of exercise every day.

Extra weight can make it hard for exotic shorthairs to breathe. So, owners should make sure their cats **exercise** every day. They should also feed cats at set times.

FAST FACT
Most exotic shorthairs need a few small meals each day.

Owners can measure out meals to make sure their cats don't overeat.

COMPREHENSION QUESTIONS

Write your answers on a separate piece of paper.

1. Write a few sentences explaining the main ideas of Chapter 2.

2. Would you like to own an exotic shorthair? Why or why not?

3. How often do exotic shorthairs need exercise?
    - A. every day
    - B. twice a week
    - C. once a month

4. Why might people in apartments want cats that don't meow often?
    - A. so the cats bother nearby people
    - B. so the cats can go outside more often
    - C. so the cats don't bother nearby people

5. What does **popular** mean in this book?

The breed quickly spread around the world. Exotic shorthairs became popular pets.

    A. common in many places
    B. not well known in many places
    C. not liked in many places

6. What does **grooming** mean in this book?

Exotic shorthairs do not need as much grooming as Persians. But their fur should still be brushed once a week.

    A. playing and exercise
    B. cleaning and caring for
    C. messing up

Answer key on page 32.

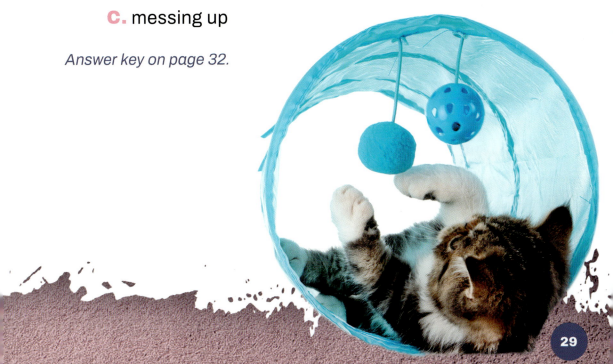

GLOSSARY

breed

A specific type of cat that has its own look and abilities.

breeders

People who raise animals to have certain looks.

exercise

To move around and stay active.

mate

To come together to have babies.

muzzles

The jaws and noses of animals.

prick

To straighten or stand up.

similar

Alike in many ways.

stain

To leave a mark on something.

TO LEARN MORE

BOOKS

Jaycox, Jaclyn. *Read All About Cats*. North Mankato, MN: Capstone Publishing, 2021.

Klukow, Mary Ellen. *Exotic Cats*. Mankato, MN: Amicus, 2020.

Pearson, Marie. *Cat Behavior*. Minneapolis: Abdo Publishing, 2024.

ONLINE RESOURCES

Visit **www.apexeditions.com** to find links and resources related to this title.

ABOUT THE AUTHOR

Abby Doty is a writer, editor, and booklover from Minnesota.

A
American shorthairs, 10

B
breathing, 19, 26
breeders, 10
breeds, 12, 14

E
exercise, 26

F
flat-faced, 19
friendly, 20
fur, 10, 13, 15, 19, 22

G
grooming, 22

M
mating, 10

N
naps, 4, 8

O
overheat, 19
owners, 4, 6, 8, 22, 25–26

P
Persian cats, 10, 12–13, 19, 22

S
shy, 20

ANSWER KEY:
1. Answers will vary; 2. Answers will vary; 3. A; 4. C; 5. A; 6. B